Planet Jupiter

ANN O. SQUIRE

Children's Press®
An Imprint of Scholastic Inc.
New York Toronto London Auckland Sydney
Mexico City New Delhi Hong Kong
Danbury, Connecticut

Content Consultant

Bryan C. Dunne
Assistant Chair, Assistant Professor, Department of Astronomy
University of Illinois at Urbana–Champaign
Urbana, Illinois

Library of Congress Cataloging-in-Publication Data
Squire, Ann.
  Planet Jupiter / Ann O. Squire.
    pages cm. — (A true book)
  Audience: Grade 4 to 6.
  Includes bibliographical references and index.
  ISBN 978-0-531-21151-9 (lib. bdg.) — ISBN 978-0-531-25357-1 (pbk.)
  1. Jupiter (Planet)—Juvenile literature. I. Title.
  QB661.S67 2014
  523.45—dc23   2013019933

All rights reserved. Published in 2014 by Children's Press, an imprint of Scholastic Inc.
Printed in China 62
SCHOLASTIC, CHILDREN'S PRESS, A TRUE BOOK™, and associated logos are trademarks and/or registered trademarks of Scholastic Inc.

1 2 3 4 5 6 7 8 9 10 R 23 22 21 20 19 18 17 16 15 14

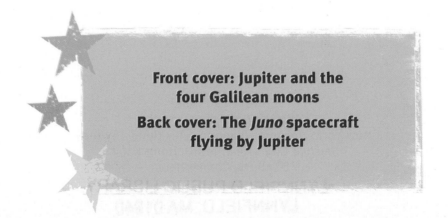

Front cover: Jupiter and the four Galilean moons

Back cover: The *Juno* spacecraft flying by Jupiter

Find the Truth!

Everything you are about to read is true *except* for one of the sentences on this page.

Which one is **TRUE**?

T or F Jupiter has more moons than any other planet in our solar system.

T or F It is likely that astronauts will someday land on Jupiter.

Find the answers in this book.

Contents

1 A Gas Giant

How is Jupiter different from planets that are closer to the sun? **7**

2 What Is Jupiter Made Of?

Why does Jupiter have stripes? **15**

3 The Moons of Jupiter

Could there be life on any of Jupiter's moons? **23**

THE **BIG** TRUTH!

The Center of the Solar System

In what ways did Galileo's discovery of Jupiter's moons change astronomy? **28**

4

Our solar system formed from a mass of dust and gases.

4 Early Views of Jupiter

Where did Jupiter's name come from? **31**

5 Exploring Jupiter

How do we hope to study Jupiter in the future? . . . **37**

True Statistics. **44**

Resources **45**

Important Words. **46**

Index **47**

About the Author. **48**

By 2014, eight spacecraft will have visited Jupiter.

Jupiter is much larger than Earth.

Earth

Jupiter

CHAPTER 1

A Gas Giant

Imagine a **planet** more massive than all the other planets, moons, and asteroids in the solar system combined. A planet whose **magnetic field** is so large it can reach beyond neighboring planets. A planet with storms that are larger than the entire planet Earth. A planet whose **gravity** is so powerful that it makes the sun wobble! Welcome to Jupiter!

Jupiter spins faster than any other planet in our solar system.

Jupiter in the Solar System

Jupiter is one of the eight planets that **orbit** our sun. It is the fifth planet from the sun, orbiting between Mars and Saturn. Unlike the planets closer to the sun, Jupiter does not have a solid surface. Mercury, Venus, Earth, and Mars are **terrestrial**. However, Jupiter is composed of liquid surrounded by gas. Humans could never land on Jupiter. There is no solid surface to land on!

This diagram shows the sun, planets, and locations of large numbers of asteroids in our solar system.

Jupiter is 2.5 times more massive than all the other planets in our solar system combined.

The Biggest Planet

Jupiter measures about 87,000 miles (140,000 kilometers) across. It is almost 11 times wider and has 300 times more **mass** than Earth. Jupiter spins faster than any other planet. It completes one rotation in less than 10 hours. Because it rotates so quickly, Jupiter is not a perfect sphere. The fast rotation causes the planet to bulge at the **equator** and flatten at the poles. Jupiter is about 5,760 miles (9,270 km) wider than it is tall.

The outer planets (the four largest planets in this picture) are called gas giants.

The Outer Planets

Jupiter is the first of the outer planets. They are the planets most distant from the sun. The other outer planets are Saturn, Uranus, and Neptune. Like Jupiter, these planets are not solid. Instead, they are composed mostly of gases or liquids. The outer planets are all much more massive than the inner, terrestrial planets. Jupiter is the largest by far.

Distance From the Sun

Jupiter's average distance from the sun is 483 million miles (777 million km). But its orbit is **elliptical**. This means Jupiter is sometimes closer to the sun and sometimes farther away. The farthest point from the sun is called the aphelion. The closest point is the perihelion. Jupiter's aphelion is 508 million miles (818 million km) from the sun. Its perihelion is 460 million miles (740 million km) from the sun.

Jupiter's orbit is the outermost ring in this drawing.

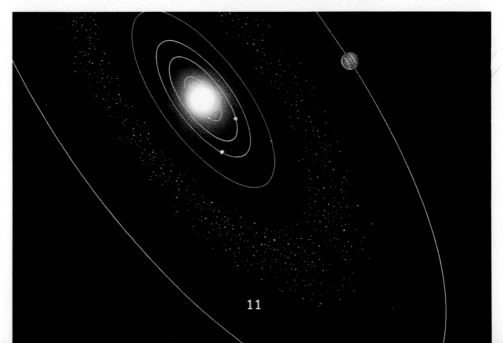

11

Distance From Earth

Earth also orbits the sun. As it does, its distance from Jupiter changes. The closest the planets come is 390 million miles (628 million km). Jupiter is easiest to see from Earth when both planets are on the same side of the sun. This happens about every 13 months. When Jupiter is on the opposite side, it is in Earth's sky during the day. Then the sun is too bright for Jupiter to be visible.

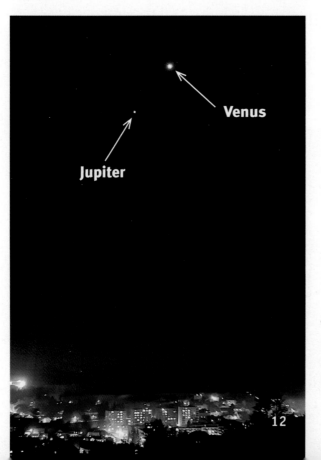

Venus

Jupiter

Venus is much closer to Earth than Jupiter is. As a result, Venus appears much brighter in Earth's sky.

12

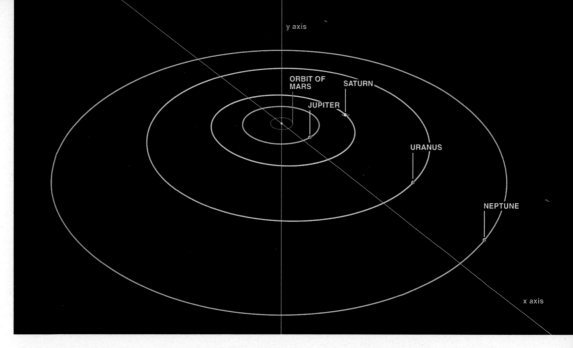

There tends to be wider distances between the orbits of the outer planets than between the orbits of the inner planets in our solar system.

Days and Years

A day is the length of time it takes for a planet to rotate once on its **axis**. Here on Earth, a day is 24 hours long. Because Jupiter makes one rotation in 9 hours and 55 minutes, a day on that planet is very short. But a year, the time it takes for a planet to orbit the sun, is very long on Jupiter. A year there is equal to nearly 12 Earth years.

Europa

 Io

Two of Jupiter's moons are shown
above the planet's outermost
cloud layer in this drawing.

Lightning

CHAPTER 2

What Is Jupiter Made Of?

Jupiter is often called a gas giant. It is composed mostly of hydrogen and helium. These are the same elements that make up the sun. But the planet isn't just a gigantic ball of gas. Most **astronomers** believe that Jupiter has a rocky or metallic **core**. A deep layer of liquid hydrogen surrounds the core. Closer to the surface, the hydrogen and helium change to gas.

Jupiter's cloud layer is about 31 miles (50 km) thick.

The Rings of Jupiter

In 1979, the *Voyager 1* spacecraft discovered that Jupiter has rings. Unlike the rings of Saturn, Jupiter's rings are very faint. The three rings are called the halo, main, and gossamer rings. They are made up of tiny particles of dust. Astronomers think that the dust comes from small meteoroids smashing into Jupiter's four innermost moons. This creates a dust cloud much like the cloud of chalk dust created when someone claps two erasers together.

This diagram shows the locations of Jupiter's rings and four of its moons.

Gossamer Rings

Main Ring

Halo Ring

Amalthea

Adrastea

Metis

16

Thebe

Jupiter's darker red stripes are clouds that are lower in the atmosphere. Whiter stripes are clouds that are higher in the atmosphere.

Jupiter's winds are about twice as strong as Earth's strongest tornadoes.

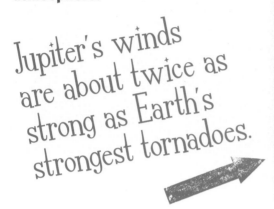

Cloudy Skies

Lying just inside of Jupiter's inner, or halo, ring are the planet's swirling clouds. They are not like Earth's puffy clouds that drift slowly across the sky. Jupiter's clouds are whipped by winds that can reach nearly 400 miles (644 km) per hour. Jupiter's stripes are actually different layers of clouds. Powerful air currents blow columns of higher, whiter clouds over the lower, redder layers of clouds.

Great Red Spot

The Great Red Spot moves among the clouds that fill Jupiter's atmosphere.

The Great Red Spot

In 1664, physicist Robert Hooke was observing Jupiter through a telescope. He noticed a large red patch on the planet. It turned out to be a huge storm. Four hundred years later, the storm is still raging. On Earth, even a strong hurricane weakens when it moves over land. On Jupiter, there is no land. This may explain why the Great Red Spot has been around for such a long time.

Jupiter's Magnetic Field

Jupiter has an incredibly strong magnetic field. It is created by energy flowing through a layer of liquid metallic hydrogen in the planet's interior. The field is so strong that it can damage instruments on spacecraft that pass by. It is larger than the sun and sometimes extends beyond the orbit of Saturn. The magnetic field also creates areas of strong **radiation**. This radiation is deadly enough to kill a human in just a few minutes.

Jupiter's magnetic field extends from its north and south poles.

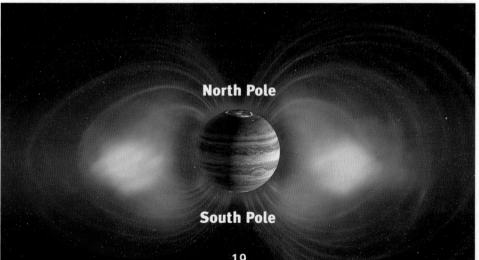

North Pole

South Pole

Gravity on Jupiter

Jupiter has the strongest gravity of any planet in the solar system. It is more than twice as strong as that on Earth. In the 1960s, Jupiter's gravitational pull captured a comet called Shoemaker-Levy 9. This brought the comet into orbit around the planet. In the 1990s, the planet's gravity broke the object into many pieces. The pieces crashed directly into the big planet. Jupiter's intense gravity even makes the sun wobble a tiny bit.

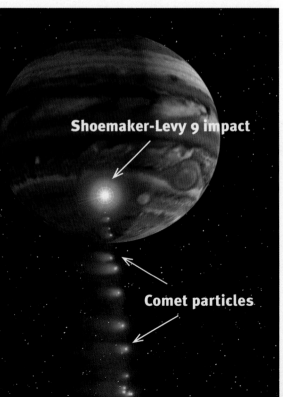

Shoemaker-Levy 9 impact

Comet particles

With the help of satellites, scientists were able to watch the pieces of Shoemaker-Levy 9 collide with Jupiter.

Scientists believe our solar system began about 5 billion years ago when a cloud of gas and dust began to collapse into a spinning disk. Most of that material came together in a dense core that is now our sun. The rest formed the planets and other objects. Astronomers think Jupiter was the first planet to form. If so, Jupiter likely influenced the formation and orbits of the other planets. Learning about Jupiter helps us understand the rest of the solar system, including Earth.

Jupiter

Io

Europa

Ganymede

Callisto

In this image, Jupiter is not drawn
to the same scale as its moons.

CHAPTER 3

The Moons of Jupiter

Jupiter has a lot of moons—67 at last count. Jupiter's strong gravity is the reason the planet has so many moons. Some were small asteroids that came too close to Jupiter and were pulled into orbit. Not all of Jupiter's moons are captured asteroids. The four largest are similar in size to Earth's moon. They are Io, Europa, Ganymede, and Callisto. These four are called the Galilean moons, in honor of their discoverer, Galileo Galilei.

Jupiter's smallest moon is only 1.2 miles (2 km) across.

Io—A Violent, Volcanic World

Io is the third largest of Jupiter's moons. It is also the closest of the Galilean moons to the big planet. Io's surface is dotted with large volcanoes. They erupt frequently, spewing out plumes of sulfur gases. These gases are what give Io its splotchy red, orange, and yellow colors. Jupiter's gravity pulls so strongly on Io that the moon's surface actually stretches. Io's rocky crust can bulge upward by more than 300 feet (91 meters)!

Red areas and dark spots mark recent volcanic activity in this photo of Io. The largest red area surrounds the volcano Pele.

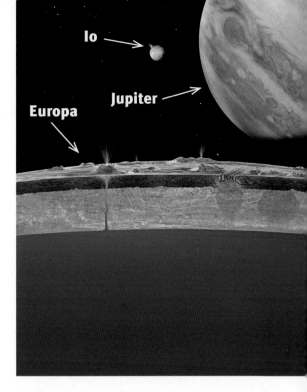

Scientists believe water sometimes bubbles up through Europa's frozen surface.

Io

Jupiter

Europa

Europa—A Smooth and Icy Moon

Europa could hardly be more different from Io. Europa is a cold, smooth moon that is totally covered by ice. Astronomers believe that below the icy crust lies an ocean of liquid water. It may be more than 60 miles (97 km) deep. Jupiter's gravity creates tides in the ocean, which cause the ice to flex and crack. These cracks can be seen on Europa's surface. Scientists believe it is possible that life exists deep in the oceans of Europa.

Ganymede (top) and Callisto (bottom) are pockmarked with craters.

Ganymede and Callisto

Ganymede and Callisto are the Galilean moons farthest from Jupiter. Ganymede is the largest moon in our solar system. It is even larger than the planet Mercury. If it orbited the sun instead of Jupiter, Ganymede would be considered a planet. Both Ganymede and Callisto are composed of a rocky, metallic core surrounded by thick layers of rock and ice. Scientists believe that both of these moons may have a layer of liquid water underneath the ice.

Discovering Jupiter's Moons

Italian astronomer Galileo Galilei discovered Jupiter's four largest moons in 1610. He was observing Jupiter through a telescope and saw what he thought were several stars near it. The next night, he was surprised to see that the "stars" had moved along with Jupiter. This told him that the objects were not stars at all, but moons orbiting Jupiter. German astronomer Simon Marius gave the moons their names.

Galileo originally went to school to study medicine.

The Center of the Solar System

Galileo's discovery of Jupiter's moons was important for several reasons. First, he used a telescope to discover objects in space that could not be seen with the naked eye. The telescope then became an important tool for astronomers.

TVBVM OPTICVM VIDES GALILÆI INVENTVM ET OPVS, QVO SOLIS MACVLAS
ET EXTIMOS IVNÆ MONTES, ET IOVIS SATELLITES, ET NOVAM QVASI
RERVM VNIVERSITATE PRIMVS DISPEXIT A. MDCIX.

Second, his discovery challenged popular ideas about how the universe worked. At that time, most people thought that everything, including the sun and planets, revolved around Earth. Galileo's discovery of moons orbiting a planet other than Earth showed that this belief might be wrong.

Galileo got into a lot of trouble for his ideas. He was put on trial and ordered to give up his beliefs. His writings were banned, and he was sentenced to prison. This sentence was later reduced, but he spent the rest of his life under house arrest, never leaving his home.

Astronomers in Istanbul measure the positions of stars and planets in the 16th century.

CHAPTER 4

Early Views of Jupiter

No one knows who first discovered Jupiter. The planet is so bright in the night sky that it is almost impossible to miss. In fact, only the sun, Earth's moon, and Venus outshine Jupiter. Every known ancient culture was familiar with the planet. In the eighth century BCE, Babylonian astronomers observed Jupiter. So did Egyptian, Chinese, Greek, and Roman astronomers.

The first astronomical observatories were built before telescopes were even invented.

Jupiter Through a Telescope

The first telescopes appeared in the early 1600s. They gave astronomers a better view of the heavens. As telescopes improved, it became possible to learn more about the stars and planets. In the 1660s, Italian astronomer Giovanni Cassini described Jupiter's colorful spots and bands. He also noticed that the planet appeared flattened. Using this observation, he made some estimates of the speed of Jupiter's rotation.

Telescopes enabled astronomers to study objects and details no one had seen before.

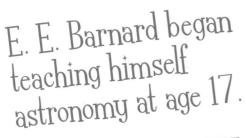

E. E. Barnard began teaching himself astronomy at age 17.

E. E. Barnard poses next to one of the telescopes at Lick Observatory in California.

Early astronomers used telescopes to discover and describe the Great Red Spot. They also learned more about the four Galilean moons. In the 1890s, American astronomer E. E. Barnard saw a fifth moon through his telescope. The moon was named Amalthea. It was the last of Jupiter's moons to be discovered by direct visual observation. Others were found indirectly through photos taken by spacecraft and telescopes.

How Jupiter Got Its Name

For centuries, there has been a tradition of naming planets after Greek and Roman gods. The Greeks named the bright planet now known as Jupiter after the king of their gods, Zeus. The Romans chose Jupiter, the king of their Roman gods. Jupiter's moons are named after the wives, children, and favorite people of the Roman god of thunder and the sky.

As the god of the sky, Jupiter was often worshipped on hilltops.

Monday, Tuesday, Wednesday, Thor's Day

Many ancient cultures named the days of the week after gods or objects in the sky. For early Romans, Thursday was Jupiter's day. The day has a similar name in languages related to ancient Rome's language. Thursday is *Jeudi* in French, *Jueves* in Spanish, and *Giovedi* in Italian. The English word comes from the Norse language, which influences English. Norse and Germanic people named the planet Jupiter for their god of thunder, Thor. Thor's Day became Thursday.

36

CHAPTER 5

Exploring Jupiter

Pioneer 10 was the first spacecraft sent to explore Jupiter and distant parts of our solar system. Launched in 1972, it reached Jupiter a year and a half later. It sent back photos of the planet and several of its moons. *Pioneer 10* kept traveling after it passed Jupiter. In 1983, it crossed the orbit of Neptune. By 2013, it was more than 10 billion miles (16 billion km) from Earth.

Pioneer 10 was launched with a plaque showing a man, a woman, and our solar system.

Voyager 1 and 2

The next spacecraft to visit Jupiter were *Voyager 1* and *2*. They passed the giant planet on their way to explore the outer solar system. The spacecraft photographed Jupiter and its moons. They discovered Jupiter's rings and Io's volcanoes. They also photographed cracks in the ice on Europa's surface. After leaving Jupiter, *Voyager 1* passed by Saturn before continuing out of the solar system. *Voyager 2* flew past Saturn, Uranus, and Neptune.

Voyager 2 reached Neptune 10 years after leaving Jupiter!

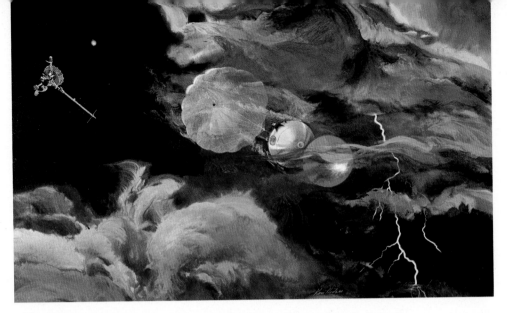

The *Galileo* probe did not survive long in Jupiter's harsh atmosphere.

Galileo

Named after Galileo Galilei, the *Galileo* spacecraft was the first spacecraft to orbit Jupiter, in 1995. *Galileo* sampled Jupiter's **atmosphere** by dropping a small probe. The probe measured temperature, pressure, level of sunlight, and several other things. Then it was destroyed by Jupiter's harsh atmosphere. *Galileo* also discovered a strong radiation belt surrounding Jupiter, as well as evidence of a vast ocean under Europa's surface.

Juno

The second spacecraft designed to orbit Jupiter was launched in 2011. *Juno* will reach the giant planet in 2016, after a journey of five years. *Juno* is equipped with solar panels so that nearly all of the energy for its six-year mission comes from the sun. Two years after its launch, *Juno* flew past Earth, using our planet's gravity as a slingshot to shoot away from the sun and toward Jupiter.

Timeline of the Study of Jupiter

1610
Galileo Galilei spots Jupiter's four largest moons.

1664
Robert Hooke first observes Jupiter's Great Red Spot.

1972
Pioneer 10 is launched and becomes the first spacecraft to fly past Jupiter.

When it reaches Jupiter, *Juno* will come as close as 3,100 miles (4,989 km) above Jupiter's cloud tops. No other spacecraft has come so near to the planet. Once in orbit, *Juno* will spend a year mapping the planet's gravity, magnetic field, and atmosphere. *Juno* will be the first mission to explore beneath the planet's dense clouds. The mission is named after the goddess Juno, Jupiter's wife, who was able to see through clouds.

2011
Juno is launched on a mission to study Jupiter's gravity, atmosphere, and magnetic field.

1995
The spacecraft *Galileo* goes into orbit around Jupiter.

2016
Juno will arrive at Jupiter.

Europa is one of the few places in our solar system where scientists believe it is possible for life to exist.

Future Missions

Future missions to Jupiter will probably focus on its moons. Water is essential for life. Scientists think life might exist in the oceans that may lie beneath the surface on Europa, Callisto, and Ganymede. The National Aeronautic and Space Administration (NASA) plans to contribute technology to a spacecraft to be launched by the European Space Agency (ESA). The spacecraft will closely observe Europa, Callisto, and Ganymede, looking for signs that life could exist on these moons.

Landing on Jupiter's Moons

What if the ESA's orbiter finds evidence that Jupiter's moons could be habitable? The next step would be to send spacecraft to land on the surface. NASA is working on an idea called the Europa Lander. This spacecraft would photograph Europa's terrain, measure temperature and radiation, and analyze samples taken from Europa's surface. It is a long shot, but the possibility that life could exist somewhere else in our solar system is too exciting to ignore! ★

Scientists want to learn more about the materials that make up Europa's surface.

Number of Earths that could fit inside the planet Jupiter: 1,300

Number of Earths that could fit inside Jupiter's Great Red Spot: Almost 2

Weight of a person at Jupiter's cloudtops: More than twice that on Earth

Speed at which *Voyager 1* is escaping our solar system, as of 2013: 915,000 mi. (1.5 million km) per day

Size of Jupiter compared to all the other planets in our solar system combined: 2.5 times more massive

Thickness of Jupiter's cloud layer: 31 mi. (50 km)

Strength of Jupiter's magnetic field, compared to Earth's: 14 times as strong

Did you find the truth?

(T) Jupiter has more moons than any other planet in our solar system.

(F) It is likely that astronauts will someday land on Jupiter.

Resources

Books

Aguilar, David A. *13 Planets: The Latest View of the Solar System*. Washington, DC: National Geographic, 2011.

Carson, Mary Kay. *Far-Out Guide to Jupiter*. Berkeley Heights, NJ: Bailey Books, 2011.

Owen, Ruth. *Jupiter*. New York: Windmill Books, 2014.

Visit this Scholastic Web site for more information on Jupiter:

★ www.factsfornow.scholastic.com

Enter the keyword **Jupiter**

Important Words

astronomers (uh-STRAH-nuh-muhrz) — scientists who study stars, planets, and space

atmosphere (AT-muhs-feer) — the mixture of gases that surrounds a planet

axis (AK-sis) — an imaginary line through the middle of an object, around which that object spins

core (KOR) — the most inner part of a planet

elliptical (i-LIP-tih-kuhl) — in a flat oval shape

equator (i-KWAY-tur) — an imaginary line around the middle of a planet or other body that is an equal distance from the north and south poles

gravity (GRAV-i-tee) – the force that pulls things toward the center of an object, such as a planet

magnetic field (mag-NET-ik FEELD) — the area around a magnetic object that has the power to attract metals

mass (MAS)—the amount of physical matter that an object contains

orbit (OR-bit) — to travel in a path around something, especially a planet or the sun

planet (PLAN-it) — a large body orbiting a star

radiation (ray-dee-AY-shuhn) — energy given off in the form of light or heat

terrestrial (tuh-RES-tree-uhl) — relating to land as distinct from air or water

Index

Page numbers in **bold** indicate illustrations

aphelion, 11
astronomers, 15, 16, 21, 25, 27, 28, **30**, 31, **32–33**
atmosphere, **14**, **17**, **18**, **39**, 41

brightness, **12**, 31, 34

Callisto (moon), 23, **26**, 42
clouds, **14**, 16, **17**, **18**, 41
colors, 17, **18**, **24**, 32
core, 15, 26
craters, **26**

days, 13, 35
distance, **11**, 12

Earth, **8**, 11, 12, 13, 17, 18, 20, 21, **29**, 31, 40
Europa (moon), 23, **25**, 38, 39, **42**, **43**

Galilean moons, 23, 24, **26**, 33
Galilei, Galileo, 23, **27**, 28–**29**, 33, 39, 40
Ganymede (moon), 23, **26**, 42
gases, 8, **10**, 15, 21, 24
gravity, 7, 20, 23, 24, 25, 40, 41
Great Red Spot, **18**, 33, 40

Io (moon), 23, **24**, 38

life, 25, 42, 43

magnetic field, 7, **19**, 41
Mars, **8**, **29**
Mercury, **8**, 26, **29**
moons, **14**, **16**, **22**, 23, **24**, **25**, **26**, **27**, 28, 29, 31, 33, 34, 37, 38, 39, 40, **42**, **43**

names, 27, 33, **34**, 35, 39, 41
Neptune, **8**, 10, 37, 38

orbits, 8, 11, 12, 13, 20, 21, **22**, 23, 27, **29**
outer planets, **10**, **13**, 38

perihelion, 11
poles, 9, **19**

radiation, 19, 39, 43
rings, **16**, 17, 38
rotation, 9, 13, 32

Saturn, **8**, 10, 19, **29**, 38
sizes, 7, **9**, **10**, 23, 26
solar system, 7, **8**, **10**, **11**, **13**, 21, **29**, 37, 38
spacecraft, 16, 19, **36**, 37, **38**, **39**, **40**–41, 42, **43**
sun, 7, **8**, 10, **11**, 12, 13, 15, 19, 20, 21, **29**, 31, 40
surface, 8, 15, **24**, **25**, 38, 39, 41, 42, **43**

telescopes, 18, 27, **28**, **32**, **33**
temperatures, 25, 39, 43
terrestrial planets, 8, 10, **13**
timeline, **40**–41

Uranus, **8**, 10, 38

Venus, **8**, **12**, **29**, 31
volcanoes, **24**, 38

water, **25**, 26, 39, 42

years, 13

About the Author

Ann O. Squire is a psychologist and an animal behaviorist. Before becoming a writer, she studied the behavior of rats, tropical fish in the Caribbean, and electric fish from central Africa. Her favorite part of being a writer is the chance to learn as much as she can about all sorts of topics. In addition to *Mars*, *Jupiter*, *Mercury*, *Neptune*, and *Saturn*, Dr. Squire has written about many different animals, from lemmings to leopards and cicadas to cheetahs. She lives in Long Island City, New York.